Fast Financial Freedom Investing in Rental Property

No Money Down! No Credit Checks! No Banks!

John Shipman

CONTENTS

Introduction

My name is John. I knew nothing about real estate when I started. My goal is to help you avoid the mistakes I made and speed up your ability to create wealth by 20 years or more.

I did everything right in life, or so I thought. I went to college. I got a degree in tech that would pay a lot. I worked in the corporate world and made a 6-figure income. Then, the recession hit. People in corporate jobs were being laid off left and right. And I was one of them. It was so devastating that people were even taking their own lives. (The ugly, but true reality of this time of desperation.)

Personally, I almost lost everything. I had to downsize to try to live off my savings. My family could no longer live the life we were used to. As I worried every day about our future and applied to numerous corporations, nothing was happening. I decided to take the last of what we had and try real estate.

I made some harsh decisions back then. Buying and renting out houses was not for me as the weight of being a landlord was costly and time-consuming. Flipping houses became physically demanding and had stressful time-constraints. I learned all I could in those days, made a lot of friends and figured out the fastest and easiest way to wealth. And I hope you can learn from what I know now.

Here is an example of someone I have met along the way. Their story is a lot like mine.

Case study-Dan

Dan Prime attended school, had outstanding grades, and then landed a solid job with perks at a reputable auto parts firm in Detroit. He believed he was having a fulfilling life.

The recession then struck his world like a cyclone. His coworkers, colleagues, and neighbors were all being laid off. Would he follow? What would he do if he lost his work to support his family? Panic overcame him. He was unable to sleep at night. Dan was going through a difficult period. However, he was fortunate in that he retained his employment throughout the ordeal.

Still, it left him with a terrible taste about the "security" of a job. His confidence in his financial future was severely damaged, and he and his wife began to formulate a Plan B. Dan and his wife devised a strategy to replace their income by purchasing one rental property every year for a decade. They chose to invest the bulk of their money and 401(k) in the purchase of these rental properties. In the wake of the recession, Detroit rents were inexpensive but still had a healthy cash flow.

In the subsequent five years, they were able to acquire five of these rental properties. Around this time, Dan's workload increased to the point where he consistently worked more than fifty hours per week and was sometimes on call after hours and on weekends.

Everyone believed his work schedule was a transitory phase, therefore he began to miss his family. One evening, after putting his four-year-old daughter to bed, she inquired whether dad had to work the next day. As he responded yes, he could see her face sink with disappointment.

This was the breaking point for Dan. He needed to expedite his ten-year retirement plan immediately, or he would miss seeing his daughter grow up. Consequently, Dan altered his real estate investment approach. Using this technique, Dan was able to pay his living costs for the following two years and leave his work. Dan has been sleeping better, eating better, and exercising since he quit his work. He is able to spend time with his family, and they travel on vacation regularly. In several respects, his connection with his wife has improved, and he is getting to know his daughter. Not having to work all day has allowed him to reflect on his life with more purpose. Dan is aware that he is now having a fulfilling life.

It Is Possible to Achieve Financial Independence Through Real Estate (but Perhaps Not in the Way You Believe)? Is Dan's tale a mere coincidence? Is Dan's method just a stroke of luck, or is there a plan at work that you can use as well?

How I met Dan?

Since I've been a full-time entrepreneur for over a decade, I've conducted podcast interviews with hundreds of successful real estate entrepreneurs. Based on my years of experience, I am certain that it is feasible to achieve financial independence via real estate. Entrepreneurs that attain financial independence are comparable to you and me. On the one hand, they want to provide for their family, but on the other, they want to govern their time. They instinctively sense that they are capable of greatness. But they recognize that in order to uncover their grandeur, they need to confront the realities of life, which is to make a livelihood. Their failure to provide for their family and manage their time frustrates them.

In contrast to most real estate investors who attend their monthly local REIA meeting, these entrepreneurs have identified a specific real estate approach that has enabled them to leave their jobs within three to five years. This method has worked for thousands in the past and will continue to work for thousands in the future, so they are convinced that it will work for you as well. Interestingly, they can do this without any prior experience and without sufficient funds to succeed. Today, these men and women have the freedom to pursue whatever interests them. They manage their own time. They spend more time with relatives. Some travel. Others continue to grow their businesses in order to leave a legacy. Because their minds are no longer absorbed by work throughout the week, these business owners may contemplate what else life has to offer. They are now able to consider a life of meaning and importance for the first time.

Financial independence is a powerful force that will transform your life and family. I'm going to introduce you to a few of these entrepreneurs and reveal the precise step-by-step Blueprint to Financial Freedom they used to achieve their goals.

This Book May Be for You If...

This book is for anybody interested in gaining financial independence via real estate. You may be seeking an escape from your nine-to-five work. It's acceptable since it pays the bills, but it's not satisfying. Or maybe you just plain dislike your work. In any case, you are seeking an exit. Perhaps you are the owner of a small firm, but the hours are killing you and dealing with staff is a nightmare. Perhaps you currently invest in single-family homes, but you're exhausted and unable to see a means to grow the company without losing your mind. You may be searching for a strategy to fund your children's education or ensure your retirement.

You're seeking passive income to eliminate the need to work (unless you want to). So that you may do anything you want, anywhere you desire, and with whoever you choose. Regardless of your position, you want financial independence. And you believe that real estate is the means to this end. You would be both correct and incorrect. Indeed, investing in real estate may lead to financial independence. But you may be mistaken because you're following the incorrect strategy—one that is not passive, will not scale, or will not help you accomplish your financial objectives. You may not agree with me at first. Or even if you do, you may not believe you can accomplish it. That is OK.

It is my responsibility to lead you in a manner that will persuade you, so that you may believe. By the end of this book, you will understand the precise technique that will enable you to achieve financial independence within the next three to five years. So, sit back, relax, educate yourself, and choose to alter your life.

Let's get this party started!

PART I
THE MOST EFFECTIVE REAL ESTATE STRATEGY FOR REACHING FINANCIAL INDEPENDENCE.

CHAPTER 1
THE INITIAL STEP TO FINANCIAL INDEPENDENCE

I will use my first apartment building investment as a case study to illustrate the profitability of apartment building investing using actual figures. And best of all, none of my personal money was used. Let me show you precisely how this trade contributed $40K to my net worth every year for five years, and I hope in the process you realize that you, too, can execute a deal like this.

Here is how I acquired the property:

- Origin: MLS (listed by residential broker)

- Price of Acquisition: $530,000

- Renovations: $54,000 (or $4,500 per apartment) - extensive renovations were required.

- Cash Required for Closing: $227,000 from 5 investors for a 50/50 split

- Projected Annual Returns: 15% for Investors

- Acquisition Charge: $15,900 due at closing

Increase rates from $595 to $825 over the following five years, and then sell the property.

After acquiring the property, I refurbished the building's façade and many flats. This enabled me to gradually increase the rate, replace vacancies, and dismiss tenants who were not paying rent. After five years, I had an agreement to sell the property for $850,000. In five years, this building generated a total profit of $198,434, or about $40,000 per year.

How is it feasible to earn $40,000 a year with such a little facility and without investing any of my own money? Let me split it down by profit center for you:

- Cash Flow: The total cash flow over five years was $130,545 (after all expenses and my fees). Approximately $181 per unit every month. As a result of increasing the average rent from $595 to $895 during the last three years, cash flow has improved over the past three years.

- Appreciation: The profit from appreciation after closure and sales charges was $146,500.

-The loan principle was lowered by $48,265 over the course of five years.

$325,310 was the entire profit from cash flow, appreciation, and debt reduction. Given that I had a 50% stake, my part of the gains was $162,655. What about the $15,900 purchase fee I am responsible for paying at closing?

It wasn't exactly rocket science. And you may do so as well.

What exactly did I do with this property? I discovered a property with issues that I believed I could resolve in three to five years with the assistance of a competent management business. I remodeled the property, raised the rentals, and decreased the vacancy rate. It wasn't exactly rocket science. Executing the strategy needed knowledge, activity, and the selection of the ideal property management firm. Just take a deep breath if you feel overwhelmed by the statistics.

Make sure you're not missing the point: Apartment complexes (even smaller ones) are the ideal method to generate passive income and long-term wealth, enabling you to achieve anything you desire within three to five years. This initial transaction dramatically altered my life since it started me on the road to financial independence. Today, I'm a full-time entrepreneur, investor, and coach, and I'm enthusiastic about helping people become financially independent in three to five years by investing in apartment building transactions with a particular emphasis on generating capital.

I am able to be with my children throughout the day and work whenever I want. I take my wife to lunch many times each week. In addition to homeschooling our children, the passive income from real estate enables our family to travel extensively. When we travel, we spend a month or two at any location we choose. But I must admit that I'm somewhat disappointed with my personal path to financial independence. It took too long and was too expensive. And it's all due of my misconceptions about apartments.

Most real estate investors never achieve financial independence because they believe they can do so by investing in single-family homes, but in reality, they cannot. In addition, many disregard apartment investment because they believe it is a sophisticated approach requiring years of knowledge and vast sums of capital. As it turns out, neither experience nor your own funds are required.

It just gets better from here.

Not only do you not need expertise or capital, but it will take you three to five years to replace your income after deciding to follow a multifamily investment approach. All of this is due to the peculiar "Law of the First Deal."

In my podcast, I've interviewed hundreds of successful real estate investors who were either financially independent or close. And I saw that their route followed a very distinct and constant pattern, which was as follows:

-Their first transaction was the smallest, most difficult, and longest to complete.

- The second and third transactions occurred in fast, almost predictable sequence.

-By the third transaction, their revenue had been replaced.

- It made no difference how large the initial trade was.

- They attained financial independence within two to three years of opting to pursue a multifamily approach.

This pattern is so persistent that I refer to it as "The Law of the First Deal," which may be articulated in the following manner:

Within three to five years following the acquisition of the first multifamily property (of ANY SIZE), financial independence is achieved. This is how effective the initial multifamily transaction is. Tyler took significant action. He took a six-month leave of absence from the government in order to purchase apartment complexes to fund his living costs. He began by using the Dave Ramsey technique for decreasing debt and cutting spending. Then, he saw a mostly unoccupied four-unit building and decided to utilize his VA loan to buy it with no down payment. He relocated his young family into one of the restored flats while he leased out the other three. He claims that he earned around $700 per month while living there for free. Upon learning about holiday rentals, he was able to raise his monthly income flow to $4,000 while his family still resided in the home. He was aware that he could only utilize his VA loan once but lacked the funds to purchase further apartment properties. Therefore, he started to solicit funds from others. He returned from a session on fundraising armed and dangerous. Using his one-deal track record, he began hunting for properties in Memphis. In fast succession, he discovered two 10- and 12-unit buildings and purchased them with the assistance of his new investors. He was living "for free" in the 4-plex, had significantly cut his living costs, and had passive income from his 26 rental units, all with no out-of-pocket expenditures. Nonetheless, he was anxious about leaving his W-2 position.

What if he had simply been fortunate? What if anything went awry? After some time, he overcame his doubts and worries and made the decision to leave his work in order to concentrate on investing full-time. Elapsed time? Eleven months since the beginning of his leave of absence. This is the force of the Law of the First Transaction: when Tyler completed his first deal, the second and third came quickly and almost automatically, and he was able to meet his living expenditures in only eleven months after he began investing.

Once Tyler was no longer employed full-time, he was allowed to consider what else he could do than work all day, every day. Through his Cash Flow Guys podcast and online content, he is now teaching people about passive income from real estate. It is all due to the Law of the First Deal.

It Took Lyle Two Years to Acquire His First Duplex, but then this occurred, Lyle started looking into real estate to offer financial stability for his family in case he lost his work and to decrease his W-2 taxes. He wanted to be a good mentor to his five children. He wanted to teach them that they don't have to spend thirty years commuting to work as he did. He wanted to instruct them on how to become entrepreneurs, property owners, and bankers. One of his kids has a learning problem, and he wanted a long-term solution to care for her. Moreover, he desired to travel more. The more he investigated real estate, the more he concluded that multifamily properties were the way to go. But he desired a modest beginning. Therefore, he researched duplexes. Numerous duplexes. Jay claims that he saw over 200 duplexes over the course of two years before deciding to purchase one. Just wanting assurance, he had to fight a great deal of tension.

He self-managed the duplex for some time before deciding he did not want to be in the management industry. He needed to acquire bigger properties in order to have a professional management firm handle everything. His primary issue was a lack of funds, so he approached his friends and relatives about investing with him.

By the time he closed on the duplex, he had an off-market commitment for 36 units in Phoenix, Arizona. It was poorly handled and broke even. So that he could refinance and repay his investors, he engaged a competent manager and started boosting the revenue.

Jay exemplifies the effectiveness of the first bargain. It took him two years to make his first investment, which was a duplex. Then, though, an intriguing event happened. The second transaction occurred very immediately after the first. And I am certain that Jay will complete his third transaction within a few months, and then he will be free of the rat race forever.

This is the effectiveness of the Law of the First Deal.

Case Study-Stan

"I Am About to Quit My Job as a Truck Driver" Stan Jacobs is a UPS driver by day, but he realized he didn't want to do that for the rest of his life, so he searched for a way out. After evaluating his choices, he concluded that multifamily investment was the way to go, but he understood he had to start small due to his low finances. Therefore, he began to search for tiny apartment complexes. He first schooled himself and then began to seek out agreements. He acquired an empty four-plex in Hagerstown, Maryland, using a hard-money loan, renovated it, and rented it out. The building's monthly cash flow was $800. He refinanced the property in order to repay the loan.

Within three months, he closed on a second investment, a five-unit property with a monthly cash flow of $1,000. How much money does he need to leave his job? Brooks need $4,000 every month, thus he is around halfway to his goal.

And he is on the verge of signing a 10-unit deal. Brooks is extremely certain that he'll be able to leave his job and become a full-time investor within the next twelve months.

Do you recognize the significance of that first deal? Even if it's a duplex or fourplex? $15,000 Monthly Passive Income from Three Transactions in Two Years.

The ONE Thing Necessary for Real Estate Financial Freedom

Gary Keller proposes in his outstanding book "The One Item" that focusing on ONE thing is the key to attaining strategic objectives. The essential question to ask in order to find the ONE thing is, "What is the ONE THING that, if accomplished, would make everything else easy or even unnecessary?"

With reference to getting financially free with real estate, the ONE thing is obviously and undoubtedly: Your first transaction. That's it. If you just remember one item from this book, remember this:

Concentrate on your first sale. Nothing else is relevant.

Put aside everything else for the time being. Focus entirely on executing your first trade. Do whatever is necessary. That is the significance of the first contract.

Therefore, this book and all my material focuses on securing that first contract. I am certain that if I can assist you with your first transaction, you will be financially independent within five years (and probably sooner). This is the effectiveness of the Law of the First Deal.

Now, you're probably thinking to yourself, "That's fantastic, John, but I don't have the cash or expertise to achieve what these guys did, especially in such a short amount of time." I had the same opinion until I personally experienced the Law of the First Deal and began to research it.

In the next chapter, I will explain the Four Secrets to Your First Deal. After learning these four secrets,

nothing will prevent you from making your first sale.
Nothing.

PART II: THE FOUR SECRETS OF A PROFITABLE APARTMENT BUILDING INVESTOR

CHAPTER TWO
HOW TO RAISE THE ENTIRE AMOUNT OF MONEY REQUIRED FOR YOUR FIRST DEAL.

When I initially recommend purchasing apartment complexes to achieve financial independence, the majority of people give me a strange look. I can see from their facial expressions that they do not think it is conceivable. And I can nearly always anticipate their next statement. It will be comparable to... "Doesn't that need hundreds of thousands of dollars?" (You don't.) However, I lack expertise in real estate investment. (Thank goodness, you do not need any.)

The reality is that you do not need thousands of dollars or expertise in real estate investment to begin apartment investing. Did you note that the entrepreneurs I presented you to began their businesses without a track record and, in the majority of cases, without their own capital? However, two to three years later, they were able to replace their income and leave their occupations.

You want to know how they accomplished this feat? There are four keys to apartment building investment success that will enable you to make your first transaction and leave the rat race within the next two to three years, even if you have no expertise or capital. This chapter is dedicated to the first of these four secrets, which is how to obtain the necessary funds for your first transaction.

The most common argument I hear from potential apartment building investors is that they lack the necessary funds. They tell me they will begin investing when they have sufficient funds. But nobody knows when this will occur. Therefore, they wait. Or they would argue that they cannot imagine entering into a contract for a construction if they do not have the necessary cash in the bank. Who will consider them credible? How will they raise the necessary funds in time to close? And how can they get funds from investors without a contract on a building? It is a catch-22, therefore they are in a bind.

When I realized there was a tremendous possibility to flip properties, I had already invested all of my money in retail businesses and had nothing left to invest. So I decided to check if any of my friends or relatives would be willing to lend me money to support these flips.

I recall receiving my first $25,000 loan from my brother-in-law. When I learned that I could flip as many properties as I want if I solicited money from people, I had a profound AHA moment. At one time, I had invested over $1 million, and over the following three years, we flipped approximately 30 properties. It turns out that I did not need my own funds after all. And neither do you.

In reality, you do not need a substantial amount of capital or strong credit to begin investing in apartment buildings. Fundraising from private folks is the alternative for getting started immediately without sufficient capital.

Why Should You Raise Funds from Others?

Here are five reasons to master the art of fund-raising:

You do not need your own funds. I hate stating the obvious, but because a lack of funds is the primary impediment to beginning apartment investment, it must be stated explicitly. To reiterate, if you receive money from investors, you are not required to utilize or have any of your own. DO NOT allow this prevent you from using the greatest real estate plan to attain financial independence.

2. You can get more deals done. Even if you have your own money to invest, you can only close so many agreements. If, on the other hand, you are able to obtain funds from other parties, your capacity to acquire real estate is limited only by your ability to identify excellent bargains. Fundraising is a talent that is highly useful to possess.

3. You can do larger deals. With the support of investors, you may pursue larger projects (and close them more quickly) than if you relied only on your own finances.

You have additional eyes on the transaction. Famous physicist Richard Feynman famously said, "The fundamental premise is that you must not deceive yourself, since you are the easiest person to deceive." When utilizing your own money, no one is watching over your shoulder, and you are thus more prone to make errors. If you can persuade people to invest in your transaction, the odds are that it is a good one.

You are helping others. People with wealth have two difficulties:

(1) They are not receiving a steady and appropriate return, and (2) they are paying excessive taxes on their earnings.

You can address both issues. You link individuals with one of the safest assets on the earth (multifamily), which gives great returns and fantastic tax advantages. You should not be hesitant to ask people for money since you are truly doing them a service. Despite their initial skepticism, they will eventually be appreciative of the opportunity you are offering for them.

You should be aware, however, of a few disadvantages of raising capital and having investors:

- You must immediately report to your superiors. You will likely be required to report to your investors in some capacity. You may be required to provide investors with updates and financial reports to keep them informed. This is far more effort than if it were just you involved. In contrast, studying Profit and Loss (P&L) accounts and sending out reports increases your focus on the transaction. Even if there are no investors, you should evaluate the reports; however, few of us have such discipline, and as a consequence, we don't pay as much attention to the investment as we should.

- You may lose some control. You may not be able to make all of the necessary judgments without investor input. As I will detail later, there are methods to limit this risk via the deal's structure.

- You will not get the whole profit. True, but as the expression goes, one hundred percent of nothing is still nothing. Great if you can purchase the whole building with your own funds. But if not, use investor funds to enter the game!

Overall, the benefits of utilizing other people's money exceed the downsides by a significant margin. This does not imply that you shouldn't use as much inventive funding as possible (especially seller financing). In conclusion, if you are excellent at soliciting funds from others, you may begin real estate investing TODAY. The Money Is Available!

When I talk to a group of real estate investors, I show how much money is available. I request that individuals raise their hands if they have a minimum of $25,000 in cash or IRA money to invest in real estate. In a gathering of one hundred, fifty individuals raise their hands. Then, I inquire who has at least $50,000, and a few dozen raise their hands. I then ask who has at least $100,000 to invest, to which a few of hands are raised.

People rapidly realize that there are far over one million dollars in the room seeking for bargains. Could you see networking with these individuals and maybe collaborating on deals you find? You bet.

The total retirement assets owned in the United States as of the first quarter of 2016 reached $24.1 trillion,? 69% of Americans, according to a 2016 poll by GO Banking Rates, have less than $1,000 in their savings accounts.

When individuals are asked whether they have money to invest, they often respond negatively. But when asked whether they had an IRA, they respond, "Of course I do... I have about $400,000." Why do you ask?"

Most individuals are unaware that they may invest with you using their IRAs. And they do so without incurring early withdrawal fees. Instead, they use the IRS tax rules that permits "self-direction" of their IRA investments. This means customers may move their IRA accounts to a "self-directed IRA custodian" and lawfully invest the funds in almost anything, including stocks, bonds, and LLCs such as your apartment complex.

Acquire a deeper understanding of self-directed IRAs and educate your prospective investors. They will initially be cautious, but they will quickly realize that investing with their IRAs is not only legal, but also one of the most effective strategies to boost their profits and build their retirement funds.

You may now agree that it makes sense to raise funds and that the funds are available. But you have a dilemma that goes something like this: "I don't have an agreement signed, therefore I can't go out and speak to investors."

That is really a difficulty.

Or, "I have a transaction under contract, but I don't have sufficient time to locate investors so I can close."

This is also a difficulty.

This catch-22 discourages the majority of real estate investors. This upsets me since it is unnecessary for this to be the case. I'm going to tell you a secret that will allow you to gather money from private folks far before you have a signed agreement. This implies that you may begin immediately. The secret is so well-kept that I have never heard it disclosed anywhere. You will be astounded by the simplicity of the secret.

Here it is then...

The Key to Fundraising Revealed

The approach to obtaining money commitments from your investors before signing your first agreement is to... Create a bargain. Huh?

You create a bargain by putting together a "Sample Deal Package." This document includes images, information on the building and neighborhood, real financials, your business strategy, and predicted financials and returns for your hypothetical transaction. This Sample Deal Package will be used when speaking with prospective investors. You will also utilize it to establish credibility with other experts you are attempting to attract for your team, such as commercial real estate brokers, bankers, insurance agents, lawyers, etc.

The difference between a Sample Offer Package and a genuine one is that the Sample Deal Package has correct information about the deal (pictures, location, financials, etc.), but you do not have a contract for it. The second distinction is that your imaginary purchase price may be lower than the asking price in order to generate the necessary returns for investors. In other words, you provide prospective investors with a transaction package that seems authentic.

How to Create Your Sample Offer Bundle

You may construct your own Sample Deal Package by following these three steps:

Obtain the marketing bundle of a building for sale as the first step. Finding a home that is being advertised for sale is the first step. This home should be comparable in size and location to the one you are seeking. It must have an effective marketing bundle (i.e., it should have photos, financials, rent roll, unit mix, and maybe some information about the area and demographics).

Multiple websites provide listings of apartment complexes for sale. Simply do a web search. I recommend using LoopNet for constructing the Sample Deal Package since it is free and simple to search. Create a free account at www.loopnet.com, log in, and search for homes that meet your requirements. Sometimes, the marketing and financial bundle may be downloaded. On occasion, you must call the broker and sign a nondisclosure agreement in order to have access to the financials. Look for a property having at least photographs, financials, a rent roll, and unit mix in its marketing package. It is advantageous if it has additional information, such as demographic data or rental and sales comps.

Step two is to develop financial predictions. The marketing bundle you downloaded should include the property's actual and expected financials. To produce ten-year financial predictions and expected returns for your investors, you will require a financial model. Incorporate cash flow, principle reduction, and future resale appreciation into your tax returns. You may either design your own or buy my Syndicated Deal Analyzer to complete the task.

I cover transaction analysis in further detail in **Secret No. 3**: How to Evaluate Transactions and Make Proposals in Ten Minutes. Once you have the 10-year financial predictions, you should copy and paste them into the Sample Deal Package.

Create the Sample Deal Package as the third step. The following is an overview of each part of the Sample Deal Package:

-Executive Synopsis This brief portion (one-half to one page) includes an explanation of the investor terms (preferred rate of return, equity, estimated returns, minimum investment, investment period), a description of the property, and an outline of the business plan (renovate and raise rents, exit strategy, etc.).

-Real Estate Information. This section offers a property description, some information about the surrounding region, and the unit mix.

-Possibility and Business Strategy. This is where you describe the issue with the property and your proposed solution. Don't worry if your financial estimates are inaccurate or if you lack all the facts. Less crucial is the accuracy of the financial statements. What matters most is that you have a compelling narrative to share. Describe the opportunities and business strategy associated with the property: maybe the rentals are below market due to ineffective management. You intend to make modest aesthetic improvements (about $2,000 per unit) and hire a competent management business. If you are able to do so, you will be able to boost rents and obtain the anticipated profits.

-Financials. This part provides the real rent rolls and financials.

-Financial Projections and Returns This part covers the financial estimates for the next five and 10 years, as well as the expected returns for your investors.

-Regarding the Management Team. Here you can see a brief biography of yourself and some of your team members, such as your property manager, attorney, and CPA. Include any more significant partners, advisers, or mentors here. This component establishes your reputation as someone who can negotiate and finish a contract.

Then What? What impact does the example Deal Package have on your fundraising initiatives? Here are the three greatest advantages:

1) It helps you see your transaction more clearly. This is essential when you increase your comfort zone by engaging in your first commercial real estate transaction or larger transactions than previously. Seeing the photographs, seeing the property, writing about it, and conversing about it bring this transaction to life for you. The more genuine it seems to you, the more at ease you get and the more assuredly you can discuss it.

2) It enables you to begin immediately. You may now plan meetings with possible investors and tell them, "I don't have a deal yet, but when I do, it will look similar to this," before presenting them with the Sample Deal Package. It provides you with something to discuss... today.

3) You will be able to get money commitments from your investors much before you have a signed contract. By the time you sign a contract on a building, you have already primed your investors and obtained money commitments based on a transaction that is basically comparable to the Sample Deal Package. When you truly have a property under contract, you will give your investors the genuine Deal Package and confirm their commitment as soon as possible.

Creating a Sample Deal Package enables you to begin apartment building investment IMMEDIATELY. It enables you to see the transaction more clearly, gives you the confidence to make bids, and gets commitments from your investors well before you place your first property under contract to ensure a timely closing.

CHAPTER 3
THE SIX STEPS TO RAISE PRIVATE CAPITAL

Now that you are aware of the Secret of Raising Private Money Using the Sample Deal Package, take these six steps to utilize the Sample Deal Package to get cash commitments from investors prior to entering into a contract:

Step 1: Create a mind map of your "Top 20" prospects.

Creating a list of individuals you know is the first stage in the fundraising process. Create bubbles on a sheet of paper for the following social groups: family, friends, neighbors, workplace, Boy Scouts, sports, hobbies, church/synagogue, etc. Then, inside each bubble, list each member of the social circle that you know. Many individuals believe they don't know anybody who may be of assistance, but after doing this mind map exercise, they are shocked to discover how many people are in their sphere of influence.

Transfer this list of individuals to a spreadsheet so you can monitor your interactions with them. The objective here is to become more deliberate in your interactions. This implies that anytime you interact with someone, you do it naturally, but if the chance presents itself, you may guide the discussion toward apartment building investment.

The mind map assists in identifying the first contact list. Choose your "top 20" prospects and initiate contact with them. Now, how can you convince these individuals to agree?

Step 2: Communicate with EVERYONE, Obtain a Sequence of YESes

Never disregard anybody; if you tell everyone you know what you want to accomplish, you will be amazed by the results. Always pursue a lead provided by someone you know. Even if this individual does not invest now, she may invest in the future or be able to suggest you to another investor.

Make sure you don't "discriminate." Often, it is difficult to determine who has money and who does not. It is astounding how much "low-key" individuals have hidden away in their IRA accounts. Likewise, it is astonishing how little money the showy banker next door has to put in anything other than his yacht and second home. Many novice syndicators make the error of attempting to get an investor's commitment too soon. Too many enthusiastic syndicators have approached their circle of influence in the following manner: "Hello, Frank! I am beginning to invest in apartment buildings and am seeking investors. The minimum investment is $25,000 and returns range from 10% to 15%. "Are you curious?"

The issue with this method is that it is too straightforward, which will likely result in a "no" and a dead end. And you have a limited number of individuals inside your sphere of influence. You want your circle of influence to expose you to as many new individuals as possible to avoid a succession of dead ends. You would want to EXPAND your sphere of influence.

Instead of immediately attempting to clinch the deal, try to meet as many individuals as possible. Focus less on the fundraising aspect and more on connection development. This is how this discussion may sound when you are speaking with a friend or acquaintance: "Hi, Frank. I am beginning to invest in residential buildings. I believe it will significantly alter the lifestyle of my family. Would you mind allowing me about five minutes to elaborate? I would love to hear your thoughts!"

Your pal will likely respond, "Yes. What is happening?" Now you have your first affirmative response. You might proceed: "That's cool. I'm seeking buildings with about fifteen apartments to purchase alongside investors. The minimum investment per investor is $25,000, and they get a 10%-15% annual return on their funds. Obviously, they can invest with cash, but they can also use their IRA or 401(k) (k). Do you know someone who would be interested in a five-minute phone conversation to discuss this further? Even if they don't have the money themselves, they may know someone who does. So, at this point, I'm simply searching for anybody who would be interested in a phone call." Your buddy may respond, "I may be interested!" Bingo, another affirmative.

Or he may respond, "Well, my boss may be." He has been talking about real estate investment, and I believe he just purchased a rental property." You: "That's fantastic. Would you feel safe asking him about a five-minute phone chat with me?" Friend: "I don't see why it would be an issue." Again, yeah. Instead of requesting a cash commitment, you are just requesting a five-minute phone conversation. Because these individuals probably know and trust you (at least to some degree), they are more inclined to suggest you to someone else they know who may be interested, even if they believe that person lacks financial resources.

Remember that you want to establish connections and increase your network. This is your first priority; fundraising comes second.

Remember the following excellent practices: - Communicate with everyone and avoid discrimination.

- Consistently request references and follow up with them.

- Include the minimum investment amount. When you invite an individual to the first meeting, you specify the minimum investment amount. If you need a minimum investment of $40,000 and the client only has $10,000 to invest, you are wasting everyone's time. Similarly, if the other party accepts the meeting, it implies that they are capable of and maybe interested in investing at that level.

Once you deem it suitable, request a meeting with the individual to discuss prospective investment opportunities.

Step #3: Ace Your First Meeting with Investors

What are your objectives for your first investor meeting? You should ideally have a cash commitment from your investor. However, you must first address their primary problem. Ensure you identify the primary risk factors associated with your proposed transaction and how you intend to minimize them. If an investor learns that this is a "unbelievably risk-free investment," they will become dubious. You will be more believable if you are forthright about the dangers and how you intend to mitigate them.

Regarding risk, ... You have two strikes against you in the eyes of the investor. First, he does not know and trust you (yet); second, you likely lack a track record (yet). You will spend most of the time establishing a rapport with the investor. Then, you may address additional arguments and detail the agreement itself (including the amount of money they'll earn).

The purpose of the meeting is to establish a rapport with the investor and convince him that you would be successful despite the absence of a portfolio of successful businesses. You may do this by discussing where you were born, your family, where you grew up, and where you attended school. Sharing such details will facilitate your connection with your possible investor. There's a good chance you'll find things you share in common.

Afterward, please discuss your professional experience. Focus on your track record of accomplishment in your professional endeavors, even if they are unrelated to real estate. Your investor should be able to see that you have a track record of success. You may transform a failure into a strength by discussing the lessons you've learnt. Discuss your passion about purchasing apartment complexes. Why are you curious? What have you achieved so far? Once you've finished talking about yourself, it's time to discuss your team; attempt to keep your remarks concise.

The focus is on your team. Discuss the property manager you hired who oversees 5,000 units in the city and specializes in rehabilitation initiatives. Mention the real estate attorney who will manage the closure and the SEC attorney who will be in charge of the syndication paperwork. Discuss the advisors and coaches on your squad.

At this point, you have done most of the talking, which is OK. You discussed your life and your enthusiasm for creating long-term riches through apartment projects for yourself and your investors. You presented your team. If you've done your job well, your investor will remark he knows you much better and is more at ease with the thought of working with you. It is now time to discuss the possibility of doing business together. Thus, your Sample Deal Package comes into play.

Here is the script:

You: I have an offer for us to consider. This building is not currently under contract, but when it is, it will resemble this in significant ways. I want your input on the terms and anticipated returns. Would that be acceptable?

[Next, discuss the executive summary page of your Sample Transaction Package with the investor, concentrating on the investor terms and not the deal itself (which occurs later)]. You: Over the life of the investment, the transaction I'm seeking should provide a return of around 13% each year. This will comprise in part of annual cash flow and appreciation. I'm seeking a minimum investment of $40,000. How intriguing would you find that? That would be intriguing to me as an investor. How long would the funds be held? You: I am advising investors to be prepared to invest their funds for at least five years. This would enable us to provide the value we want. What would your opinion be? Investor: That is OK. Would there be any distributions of cash flow? You: Yes. We will typically pay out payments quarterly. How does it sound to you? Investor: That seems plausible. What do you consider the biggest dangers to be? You: It would depend on the transaction, but I believe our ability to execute our business strategy represents our largest risk. We may not attain the planned returns, or it may take longer than anticipated. For instance, suppose our strategy calls for renovating 50 percent of the apartments in order to increase rents by 20 percent. We would ensure that sufficient funds are in the bank account to cover the improvements. However, it is possible that the renters would not go as soon as anticipated, therefore it may take longer to increase the rates. However, my objective for the first few homes we acquire will be to minimize these types of risks. In other words, I do not want an empty building or a structure with several issues. I will search for a decent price on a pretty stable structure. Before we examine the Deal Package, I will discuss the concept in further depth and highlight the risks so that you can make a more informed choice once I have a building under contract. What further questions or concerns do you have concerning the returns and conditions we have discussed so far?

The investor should now feel somewhat at ease with you as a person, as well as with the risks, rewards, and conditions of the transaction. Do not make investors believe that your conditions are fixed in stone if you are just beginning to speak with them. Instead, collect information from your investors on what they would like (and would not like) if they invested with you. Examine the Sample Deal Package itself next. However, do not waste too much time, since there is likely not much time remaining in the meeting. Although the figures are hypothetical, they should offer the investor a sense of the kind of transaction you're seeking. You: Let's take a moment to examine the Deal Package. As previously said, this is not a transaction for which I am presently under contract. However, when I do, it will resemble this. [Then, quickly review each element of the Deal Package to orient the investor and respond to any queries. Since numbers are subject to change, you should not concentrate on them.

Finally, you should conclude by explaining the investor's viewpoint on the mechanics of concluding a transaction. You: I am grateful for your time today! This is what will occur next. When a property is under contract, I will send you the Deal Package via email. If you are interested in investing, please let me know the amount you are contemplating, and I will advise the attorney to initiate the closing procedure if the investors and due diligence are suitable. You will get a Private Placement Memorandum and an LLC Operating Agreement. You sign both the Operating Agreement and a subscription agreement detailing the amount of the investment. A day or two before closing, you wire the closing attorney the monies. Initially, I want to give a monthly email report to investors, and after things have settled, I will issue quarterly updates along with any dividends. What worries or questions do you have about this?

Give them the Sample Deal Package to take home and arrange a phone call or meeting to address any questions or concerns. Don't miss this step! Ensure you address their issues immediately, while there is still time, as opposed to waiting until you have a signed agreement and time is of importance. If you follow this procedure, you will be shocked at how fast you can get investor commitments after you have a contract in place. This will give you the confidence to make bids on houses and acquire the closing monies in a timely manner.

Step 4: Maintain contact.

After this first encounter, it is essential to maintain contact with the investor. Hopefully, you have planned the first follow-up call or meeting. Ask them once again whether they're okay proceeding if you've located the ideal offer. It is crucial to maintain contact with the investor after the second meeting, since you cannot predict how long it will be before you close a contract.

At least once a month, offer an update and inquire about what's new in his or her life. Consider adding all of your possible investors to an email list (such as MailChimp) and sending them a monthly newsletter or similar communication. Thus, they will be prepared to address any questions or concerns they may have.

Ask them once again whether they're okay proceeding if you've located the ideal offer. It is crucial to maintain contact with the investor after the second meeting, since you cannot predict how long it will be before you close a contract. At least once a month, offer an update and inquire about what's new in his or her life. Consider adding all of your possible investors to an email list (such as MailChimp) and sending them a monthly newsletter or similar communication. Thus, people will anticipate hearing from you, and you will have established a mechanism for maintaining contact.

Step 5: Sign a "Letter of Intent to Invest"

I utilize what I call a "Letter of Intent to Invest" whenever an investor orally agrees to a certain cash amount. It is a brief, one-page document that is not legally enforceable but "formalizes" the pledge. A pleasant bonus is that it may serve as a "Proof of Funds" letter when you're making bids in the future.

Once you have contacted everyone in your immediate circle of influence (and continue to maintain those connections), it is time to expand your network. Here are three suggestions for expanding your network of possible investors:

- First tip: warm up cold contacts. Examine your contacts list in Gmail, Outlook, or whatever address book you use. You probably have hundreds of connections but have lost contact with the majority of them. Before deleting cold contacts, maybe there is a method to reconnect with them. Import your cold contacts into a mailing service application, such as MailChimp. Send a first email apologizing for how poor your communication has been. Give them a basic update about your life and inquire about theirs. You will be astonished by how many individuals are eager to hear from you. There is a fresh list of warm connections.

Continue communicating with these new acquaintances in a natural manner (i.e., don't beg for money, but rather reconnect). This might take weeks or even months. Be patient. Continue delivering a monthly update to the remaining contacts who did not answer. You may be more deliberate about your apartment building efforts in future interactions so that people learn to recognize you in that context. Continue this procedure until the individual unsubscribes from your newsletter or you reconnect. A inexpensive and simple method for expanding your network!

- Tip 2: Attend local real estate events to network. Local REIAs are one of the finest places to meet prospective investors. You must attend all REIAs within a reasonable driving distance. Additionally, search meetup.com for local real estate meetings. If there aren't any in your region, you should try forming one. You should aim to attend one networking event weekly.

- Tip No. 3: Use Bigger Pockets to network. Bigger Pockets is perhaps the biggest online real estate investing community. You may search for members in your region and send them a personal message if you are a Pro member. Start a discussion online, invite them to a local meeting, or create a new group for members. There are several opportunities to meet new individuals. Be inventive and consistent in your efforts to meet new individuals.

The Key to Fundraising Is a Game-Changer. What impact does this have on your capacity to begin investing in apartment buildings? It makes an enormous impact. If you apply my Secret to Raising Money and follow the techniques explained in this chapter, you may have verbal commitments from investors before your first agreement is signed. Wouldn't it help you to make more confident offers? Of course. It would provide you with a LOT of confidence.

Imagine you have five investors who have agreed to investing $40,000 with you if the transaction matches the Sample Deal Package. Behind you is $200,000 in cash. Wouldn't that affect how you communicate with brokers and sellers? And if you have a contract for a genuine transaction, wouldn't it take you just a few days to acquire the necessary funds to close? Yes, indeed.

Herein lies the strength of the Secret to Fundraising. Utilize it to create confident offerings. Utilize it to quickly generate funds. Now you understand how to raise the funds necessary to complete your first transaction. This brings us to the following secret: how to get your offers approved without Proof of Funds, even if you're a beginner.

How to Get Your Offer Accepted Without Experience or Proof of Funds, Secret No. 2 of Chapter 3

Lack of expertise is one of the most common reasons why individuals hesitate to invest in apartment buildings. They believe they need years of experience investing in single-family homes before they can "graduate" to multifamily.

I recall the first time I called brokers. The broker wanted me to email him a Proof of Funds along with my apartment investing résumé after we had hardly spoken. This often terminated the discussion, and the broker never called back again. I would say the following to a broker: "Hello, my name is John, and I'm interested in investing in multifamily buildings with a minimum return of 10%. Can you email me a list of offers?" It took me some time to figure out what was going on since I was clueless. I was making several errors that prevented me from getting into the game. The response was not that I needed further experience. I had to establish my credibility.

To teach you this second secret of how to have your offer approved without experience or Proof of Funds, I must demonstrate how to avoid making the same errors I did. Even if you lack real estate expertise, I will provide you with four pointers to avoid making these errors. This will ensure that you are treated seriously.

Educate yourself so that you do not seem like a novice.

There is specialized terminology used by commercial real estate professionals. Evidently, I wasn't using the correct terminology (or wasn't using them correctly), and others quickly categorized me as a novice. The greatest way to prevent this error is via education. When speaking with other professionals, you must use the appropriate terminology, and you only have one opportunity to create a good impression. Therefore, if you phone a broker and appear inexperienced, it will be tough to establish your reputation. When the broker asks you the following questions, you know you sound like a novice.

Before I can provide you the financial documents, the vendor needs a Proof of Funds.

Which multifamily experience do you possess?

Since I was not utilizing the correct wording in my script when phoning brokers, I was not proactively addressing the primary issue of every broker who receives a call from a new investor: Could I close? In other words, did I have the appropriate funds and experience?

When I made cold calls to those brokers, this is what was going through their minds. They pondered whether they should take me seriously or if I was wasting their time. This example script will prevent you from sounding unprofessional: "I work with a group of affluent people, and we would want to enter the Chicago market. We have already recruited XYZ property management firm and are continuing to develop our workforce. We are seeking steady value-add agreements in the $1M-$2.5M area with a minimum 8% cap rate, but no repositioning opportunities. Is there anything you can provide for me to evaluate that you have in the works?"

Here is what you did:

You addressed the financial aspect by stating that you deal with wealthy folks.

You answered the experience requirement since you are working with a property management firm and you state that you are "growing," meaning that you have experience.

You use terminology like cap rate, consistent value-add, and reposition, which are exclusive to commercial real estate professionals.

Do you see how a little script modification may make a significant difference? This is only one illustration of how education may provide substantial returns. Ensure that you educate yourself! There is a wealth of free resources to help you get started, but if you're serious, you'll need to invest in your education.

Join Bigger Pockets and read every apartment investing-related blog article and forum thread.

- **Listen to all podcasts on apartment building investment.**

-**Read each and every book on apartment building investment.**

-If you have exhausted all free resources and want to go further, it may be time to invest in your education. Purchase an online course, attend a seminar, and/or retain the services of a coach.

-Build your team so that you do not seem inexperienced.

The second error I made was not having a competent staff supporting me. I was unable to answer the question of who would manage the building since I had not yet engaged a property management business. Investors inquired about the attorney who would handle the deal, but I did not have one. Brokers inquired as to who my lender was, and I did not have one either. Nothing about this enhanced my credibility. To prevent this error, surround yourself with those who possess the knowledge you lack. If you have a solid team around you, it becomes less about you (and your lack of experience) and more about the team's combined experience and track record.

Imagine a discussion with a skeptical broker who inquires about your experience. With a competent team, you may be able to respond to his queries like follows: You: Sure. Sam at XYZ property management, who oversees 5,000 units in town and specializes in the kind of value-add agreements I seek, is on board. Are you acquainted with Don? Sure, he's a fantastic man. He knows exactly what he's doing! You: He really does. Jack Jones handles the details of the closing for me, and I'm dealing with Wanda at Shaker Bay for the financing. I have completed many transactions with Jack. He is excellent and responsive. Wanda is from Chicago, correct? You: That is correct She has also originated multiple loans for Sean Jones, one of the consultants on my team.

WOW. Is this not a very different conversation? Do you not believe that this would assuage anyone's concerns about your lack of experience?

Your property manager is the first and most essential team member to hire. He or she has the experience you need and can instantly establish your reputation. I referred to a "board of advisors." This may include one or more seasoned multifamily investors who agree to serve as your resource. This might be a paid or unpaid mentor or coach. For instance, you may discover possible advisers via your local REIA, meetings, and Bigger Pockets.

Be professional to make a favorable first impression.

You do not sound like a novice, and you are supported by an experienced crew. Thirdly, to be regarded seriously, you should seem "professional." This is an easy task that will have a significant impact. Here are a few suggestions for establishing a professional first impression:

- **Form an LLC.** It is more professional to operate as a business rather than as an individual. Choose a catchy name and complete the necessary papers to register the LLC. Typically, you can do this yourself for little cost by studying online the requirements in your state. In addition to seeming more professional, you may deduct business costs.

-Purchase business cards. It seems more professional if you have a business card to offer to someone. It is simple and inexpensive to do this yourself. You may pay someone on Fiverr to create a logo, and then use any of the available online services to design and print business cards.

- Construct a website. This is more difficult if you're not very tech-savvy, but it's easier than ever before. Investigate the websites of different apartment building investors to see which ones you like. I recommend beginning with a single-page website since it is simpler and adequate.

Regarding the matter of seeming professional, I have seen students get trapped in this phase due to their perfectionism and fear of moving on to the next step, which is making offers. Please note that this step is entirely optional! You don't need business cards and a website to be considered seriously; they're just helpful tools for enhancing your professional impression. If you can do them in a week or two, that's fantastic. But if this process would consume weeks of your time, you should outsource it or omit it.

Step 6: Make Incredible Offers!

My second major error was making proposals that were not taken seriously. The majority of answers to my proposals requested my profile and Proof of Funds. I was not accepted to the game since I was unable to pass the gatekeeper. Now that you've educated yourself, collected an experienced team, and presented yourself in a professional manner, it's time to submit an offer that catches the broker's eye.

The submission of a Letter of Intent (LOI) to make an offer is a solid first step, but it's not sufficient, particularly when you're just getting started. It does not provide you sufficient credibility and does not make your offer compelling enough. Even though the broker now regards you as a prospective purchaser, he must make your offer to the seller. And if the seller is not persuaded that you can close, they will not accept your offer, even if it is larger than the amount offered by other purchasers.

When making an offer, you should put your best foot forward. The following elements are crucial for constructing a solid Offer Package:

- **The Offer Cover Letter.** The Offer Package should begin with a one-page Cover Letter that introduces you, your offer, and your extended team.

- **Letter of Intention (LOI).** Follow the Cover Letter with the Letter of Intent, which includes the conditions of your offer, including price, down payment, and closing date. This serves as the foundation for the negotiation. After you and the seller have signed the LOI, you may have your attorney create the purchase agreement.

The Effect: Immediate Credibility with the Individuals You Meet

By adhering to these four guidelines, you will use the appropriate terminology, discuss your team, and provide a professional first impression. And you're combining everything into a product that is taken seriously. Do you behave like a novice? No, certainly not. You exhibit the demeanor of someone who understands what they're doing. Will you fib about your inexperience? No, certainly not. You will accept it (if questioned) and mention your team, your firm, and your enthusiasm for closing your first contract.

I can tell you that if you do these things, the likelihood of being questioned about your experience is quite minimal. Because you just pretend to possess experience. In addition, a broker will not risk insulting you by asking you this question. What if you owned hundreds of units already? You may get rather angry with the broker if he or she requires you to defend the phone calls you are now conducting. Brokers are intelligent, and they will avoid offending a possible customer.

You may be thinking: That's fantastic, John. I can see how I may look more knowledgeable than I really am. However, what if the broker requests Proof of Funds? What If I'm Asked for a Letter of Proof of Funds? In reality, it is uncommon to be requested for Proof of Funds if you use proper language and project confidence.

When I asked Martha Dugan whether she need a Proof of Funds letter before she signed his first contract, she said, "John, to answer your question, I have not been requested for Proof of Funds." Your training raised my confidence tremendously, and I used your scripts, so Proof of Funds was never an issue. I recently had my first bid for an 80-unit transaction accepted, and I am now negotiating the contract.

Peter Gray noted that she first struggled with the Proof of Funds question: I recently began working with John and have made many proposals. In the beginning, the brokers gave me a difficult time and demanded Proof of Funds. However, after a few weeks they stopped asking. In fact, my first Letter of Intent for a 50-unit purchase was recently accepted. I'm delighted to do my first transaction!

These inquiries concerning track record and Proof of Funds indicate that you sound like a beginner. In order to be regarded seriously by brokers and investors, you must educate yourself, improve your talents, and create your team.

If you sound and seem confident, the likelihood that you will be requested for a Proof of Funds letter is minimal. That said, it's normal to still be nervous about being asked. Not to fret. I will demonstrate three methods to respond to a request for Proof of Funds when you have none.

How to Respond to Requests for Proof of Funds When You Have None

The difficulty is that if you are raising capital, you likely do not have the liquid assets or net worth to fulfill a seller's need for Proof of Funds. You do not already have the monies in a bank account as a syndicator. You will raise the funds from others and put them into an escrow account prior to closing. However, you do not own it right now. It might be difficult to convince a seller to sign a contract with you. Even if you look assured, the broker and/or seller may want Proof of Funds (POF) on occasion. This can be a significant issue that you must know how to address.

While presenting the seller with actual Proof of Funds would certainly satisfy them, there are other steps you can take beforehand. Here are three guidelines to follow when you are asked to provide Proof of Funds:

First tip: push back.

A request for Proof of Funds demonstrates a lack of confidence. If the seller was confident in your ability to close, they would not request this. First, you should respond with something like, "I understand that you are concerned about our ability to close given that we will be raising capital." However, I already have verbal commitments from my investors for the necessary funds to complete the transaction. It will be in the escrow account at closing, but I do not currently have it in a bank account. I cannot provide you with Proof of Funds. What about this though? Why don't we get together and become acquainted? If you do not feel 100 percent comfortable proceeding with us, we will part as friends. What do you say? If you're feeling gutsy, you could add: If your seller insists on Proof of Funds, we're going to have to move on. I have another four deals I need to look at today.

People do business with people they like and trust. The best way to build trust is with an in-person meeting with the broker and/or the seller. This gives you a chance to build rapport, tell them what you've done and what you want to accomplish, and then present them to your team members. If you are unable to see the broker or seller in person, you will need to do business remotely by phone call and email. If email is the only option, develop a Cover Letter that includes a summary of your successes and how you plan to raise funds to close the contract. Include your biography and the investment package for this business venture. Make the seller as comfortable as possible with the thought of continuing the transaction. If Tip #1 fails and you still choose to proceed with the transaction, the following two recommendations will help you fulfill the seller's requirement for Proof of Funds.

Indicating your investors' desire to invest is the second tip.

In lieu of an actual Proof of Funds, you may also provide the seller with Letters of Intent to Invest (which we discussed in "The Six Steps to Raising Private Money"), signed by each investor and indicating the amount they are interested in contributing. This often satisfies the seller, and for the investors, it is in no way legally binding and costs them nothing to sign. However, it significantly enhances the credibility of your cause.

Receive Proof of Funds from one of your investors as the third tip.

Obtaining a Proof of Funds from one of your investors is a third alternative if Tip No. 2 fails to sway an unyielding seller and you're determined to proceed with the transaction. Proof of Funds may be shown in several ways: It might be either a bank or brokerage statement or a letter from the investor's banker or broker. Frequently, investors prefer the latter since it does not reveal the actual amount they have, but rather affirms the amount you must display. A Proof of Funds letter or statement is provided at no cost to the investor. It is not legally binding and the investor is not required to invest any money. Therefore, there is no responsibility on the side of the investor. If you're having trouble obtaining a POF letter from one of your investors, you may spend $5 to COGO Capital to get one for up to $500,000. (more if you contact them). Google "COGO Capital Proof of Funds" to get the PDF letter.

Typically, sophisticated brokers will not accept this, but the Proof of Funds letter is a formality or "checkbox" that will frequently suffice.

Make the Proof of Funds contingent on the Letter of Intent being signed.

If you must present Proof of Funds in order to proceed, demand that it be contingent on a signed Letter of Intent. Include the phrase "Proof of Funds within 48 hours after ratifying the LOI" in your letter of intent. Explain to the broker or seller that you can get the Proof of Funds letter, but that your investor wants to confirm the legitimacy of the transaction before contacting their banking institution. A signed Letter of Intent is the strongest indicator that an agreement is "genuine."

I hope you now see how these methods might make you look more knowledgeable than you really are. You have educated yourself in order to use the proper terminology. You've assembled a team to compensate for your lack of expertise, and you describe yourself in terms of this group. You've established a business and website that convey a professional first impression. And you use this information to create proposals that will be approved.

Now that the problem of experience has been handled, all you need to know is how to assess opportunities and make offers. This may seem intimidating, but I'll demonstrate how to do it in about 10 minutes.

CHAPTER 4
HOW TO ANALYZE DEALS AND MAKE OFFERS WITHIN TEN MINUTES.

Real estate is a game of numbers. The more offers you make, the more transactions you conclude. The issue is that studying apartment complex transactions may be time-consuming, limiting your capacity to make several bids. When I initially began, I felt absolutely overwhelmed. I would get a marketing package from a broker and input the financials into a spreadsheet I had built in order to do mathematical calculations. I would then make a few phone calls and do internet research. I spent four hours analyzing a deal and submitting an offer. Four hours! As you can guess, I was unable to make many proposals; in fact, I almost quit since I was overwhelmed and unable to do the task quickly enough. Previously, I lacked the tools and approaches I possess today. I subsequently identified a superior method. I call it the "10-Minute Offer," and it allows you to make an offer on a broker's deal within ten minutes of receiving the marketing materials. It is that effective, and it will expedite your progress toward your first transaction.

Now, a word of caution: The 10-Minute Offer contains some numbers and rudimentary arithmetic, but if your eyes begin to glaze over, just continue reading. Continue reading even if you don't comprehend everything immediately. Okay, let's immediately begin the 10-Minute Offer.

The 10-Minute Proposal

Step 1: Adjust the Income - four minutes.

If the marketing materials include real financials, search for "Gross Scheduled Income." This is the amount of revenue that would be expected if all units were occupied, and rents were set at market rates. Simply use this number for the 10-Minute Offer. Examine the changes for vacancies, concessions, bad debt, etc. If these modifications are larger than 10%, use that figure as the vacancy factor; otherwise, use 10%. If you just have pro-forma financials (i.e., what the financials would be if the property were managed effectively), then you should utilize those statistics. Now, your Adjusted Income equals Gross Scheduled Income minus 10%.

Step 2: Modify the Expenses (three minutes)

This will be a simple task. If the reported or projected costs exceed 55%, use that percentage; otherwise, use 55%. That sum is your Adjusted Expenses. When stated costs are less than 55%, something is often missing. For instance, the management costs may not be included since the current owner manages the property on his or her own. Spend little time evaluating this, but examine if there are any evident expenses missing from the broker's marketing materials. This will be your case for why the expenditures are unreasonably low. Now you may compute the Net Operating Income Adjusted: Adjusted Net Operating Income (NOI) is Adjusted Revenue minus Adjusted Expenses.

Step #3: Utilize the Advertised Capitalization Rate to Calculate a Revised Fair Market Value—3 Minutes

Typically, the marketing materials for a property include the Cap Rate, or your broker will inform you of the Cap Rate used to establish the asking price. If the Cap Rate is unclear, you may rapidly determine it using the following formula: Capitalization Rate = Net Operating Profit / List Price Make a note of the Cap Rate, as you will soon use it to your advantage. Now that we have the Capitalization Rate and Net Operating Income, we can compute the Adjusted Value using the following formula: Value Adjusted = Net Operating Income Adjusted / Capitalization Rate Here is an example. Assume the asking price is $653,00, the income is $95,000, and the costs are $42,750. After using the 10-Minute Offer method, the Adjusted Value is $506,250.

In most cases, the Adjusted Value will be less than the asking price since the revenue and costs in the marketing package were initially unduly optimistic! In this case, the asking price is $653,000, but the adjusted value is $506,000 since the reported income was high and the reported costs were lower than our standard. Notate the revised price, and let's return to the broker.

Step #4: Send Your Analysis and Informal Offer Price to the Broker

Compose an email to the broker detailing the modifications you made to the income and costs. Explain that after using the broker's Cap Rate, the adjusted price is X and that you would be willing to make an offer at that amount if the seller is agreeable. Send your broker a message similar as this:

Hello, Bob I examined the shipment you sent me. Everything seems to be in order, just as we discussed over the phone. However, I made a few modifications to the underwriting. Due to the lack of real financials, I had to depend on the given pro forma data. We both recognize that they will be lower than actuals, correct? At the time, this is all we have to work with. In your pro forma, vacancies accounted for 5% of the Gross Potential Rent, which, in my experience, is generally closer to 10% when bad debt, etc. is included in. Regarding expenditures, I do not know the real figures, but the pro forma totals amount to less than 45% of revenue. For instance, it looks that the insurance expenditures are absent, and the P&L allocates a little amount for repairs. Based on previous knowledge and real financials for comparable listings in the region, I am aware that they are extremely low. I generally use 55% of the money for the costs, and that's what I'm doing here. You are advertising a Cap Rate of 8% for this investment. I'm not sure whether that's fair for this location, but let's pretend it is. If you use an 8% Cap Rate to the Adjusted Net Operating Income, the value of the facility is just about $500K, quite a ways away from the $650K asking price. If you see an error in my underwriting, please let me know. I could make an offer at the asking price, but I don't want to waste your time if we both know that the real NOI will be lower than the pro forma after due diligence is performed. I like to be more realistic up front. I don't know how flexible your seller is on the asking price, but I'd be willing to make an offer of $500,000 if he's willing to consider it. Please let me know your thoughts. I forward hearing from you.

That is all! This is how to do an analysis and make an offer in 10 minutes.

Do not spend your time examining transactions. Work smarter, not harder. If you do, you'll be able to examine more offers and have a greater chance of discovering one that works. Because you won't sound like a beginner, your confidence will rise, and you'll be able to make more offers, learning to assess transactions is the most critical skill to acquire early on.

CHAPTER 5
THE NUMBER ONE WAY TO
LOCATE THE BEST DEALS

You may be thinking, "Yes, I get that deal analysis is a crucial ability, but isn't it difficult to locate excellent bargains right now?" Deals will not just fall into your lap. You are aware that real estate is a numbers game, right? The more offers you make, the sooner you will complete your first transaction. And now that you know how to make an offer in 10 minutes, you may swiftly make several offers. Certain gurus will demonstrate how to promote estates, send yellow letters to apartment owners, and network with lawyers. All of these strategies may be effective, but I've found that they need time and money.

There is a superior method that can bring you the finest discounts more quickly and with less effort.

The Number One Way to Locate Apartment Building Deals

A solid network of commercial real estate (CRE) brokers is the most effective and time-saving approach to locate outstanding apartment building discounts. CRE brokers are in the business of locating transactions. The superior ones write postcards and letters to apartment building owners and cultivate relationships with them years before a seller is ready to sell. They engage in significant networking and footwork to get listings and buyers. The local Marcus & Millichap broker would routinely check in with me every three months for years. They would sometimes offer to take me out to lunch or do an informal "appraisal" of my buildings to determine their value. No conditions attached. This person is smart: he may not obtain a listing today, but he could in the future, or I might purchase one of his properties. Unfortunately, the majority of brokers are subpar. The few good ones are worth their weight in gold, and you only need a few to have an endless supply of fantastic offers.

I recall marketing for deals in Chicago in 2007 after attending my first apartment building boot camp. While I did send out letters (a lot of labor, and I did not close a single sale after many months of marketing!), I mostly concentrated on cold phoning CRE brokers. Over the course of many weeks, I observed that a few brokers genuinely took me seriously and had frequent dealings. Moreover, they communicated regularly, unlike other brokers. I discovered one broker who supplied me with virtually weekly offers.

Concentrate your efforts on locating two to three brokers who are prolific deal-makers and who take you seriously, and you will be set for the remainder of your real estate investment career.

How Do You Locate Reputable CRE Brokers? LoopNet is one of the finest methods to locate prospective brokers to deal with. I hear you saying, "LoopNet is useless for finding transactions," which is mostly accurate, but it is a gold mine for locating CRE brokers. Here is the method I use to locate CRE brokers on www.LoopNet.com (creating an account is free).

I look for the kind of properties I want to acquire. I populate a spreadsheet with the contact information of all CRE brokers with listings. After completing many transactions, I encounter the same brokers again, and I keep note of how many listings each broker has. More listings are preferable. I then make cold calls to the brokers using the script in Tip No. 1: Educate Yourself to Avoid Sounding Like a Novice.

If the bargain on LoopNet doesn't exactly fit my profile, I write something along the lines of, "I noticed your listing on LoopNet, but that deal doesn't quite work for me. What more do you have?" I may tell the broker what I'm searching for and learn a bit about him or her, too. Then, I observe the broker's trade flow and how he or she communicates with me.

A face-to-face encounter is a suitable next step if you believe the broker is among the best. I keep track of all of these activities in an Excel spreadsheet. Over time, a few brokers will rise to the top.

Working with Brokers to Maintain Deal Flow: Three Tips

Many brokers will not even email you a bargain when they have one, making them shockingly tough to work with. Therefore, you are responsible for ensuring that your partnership is as fruitful as possible. Here are three methods I've found useful for keeping a continuous transaction flow from your broker network.

Tip #1: Be persistent. The majority of brokers will not react to your first contact effort. Typically, I send a series of emails, phone calls, and text messages before receiving a response. If you do not get a response after three to five tries, it is time to remove that broker from your list and move on.

Tip #2: Be responsive. When a broker delivers you a deal, you must react within forty-eight hours with your comments. And when I say "feedback," I mean you're offering them an informal 10-Minute Offer for every sale that you receive. My brokers have informed me that just approximately 25% of their buyers respond to their inquiries. If you're responsive, you quickly float up to the top of their buyer's list. Another advantage of responsiveness is that the broker knows what kind of transactions you want and dislike.

Tip #3. Maintain consistency Keep in contact with your brokers often. Send them an email, text message, or voicemail once every two to four weeks to remind them that you're still around. Remind them of the terms of the offer or send them a blog post or news piece that may be of assistance.

"Off-Market" listings are the Holy Grail of working with brokers.

You regularly and swiftly communicate with brokers, and you may meet them in person for lunch or a property tour. Over time, the broker will recognize you as a serious buyer since he or she will know precisely the kind of transaction you want. When the real estate agent is working on a new property, he may phone you and say, "Hey, I'm working on a new listing. I believe it fulfills the description of what you're seeking. I will provide you the rent roll and financials, but I will not have the listing signed and the marketing package available for another 10 days. Examine it and choose whether you want to make an offer before it goes on the market."

What just transpired? You have just acquired an off-market transaction, commonly known as a "pocket listing," since the broker has not yet advertised the item to the general public. In other words, you are not competing with the whole globe for this one transaction. This is the holy grail of broker relationships: gaining the confidence of your brokers and becoming one of their favored purchasers so that they will offer you off-market prospects before anybody else. It will take some time to reach this destination, so please be patient. But once you reach that point (and you will!), you will have as many transactions as you can manage with only one or two competent brokers.

Other Ways to Locate Discounts

Finding offers via brokers is the most effective means of doing so. But if you need additional transaction flow and you already know every broker in town, consider the following: Real estate managers. Property managers may be an excellent source of discounts. They have an intimate knowledge of their properties and are often the first to know when the owner is ready to sell. As you expand your team by networking with property managers, regularly inquire whether any of their owners are interested in selling.

Direct mail

Sending letters to apartment owners is another means of generating leads. You may acquire lists from list brokers such as listsource.com and have the letters printed and sent for you (like YellowLetters.com). The downside of direct mail is that it is costly, time-consuming, and has a variable response rate. Due to the small number of apartment owners in each city, it is feasible to send them a letter every three months on a budget.

Condominium Owners Association

Joining an Apartment Owners Association is an excellent way to network. This is where other owners congregate, and it's an excellent method to identify possible sellers, buyers, partners, and other specialists who can assist you.

Driving

Driving for money might also have results. A run-down complex is an indication that it is mismanaged and has difficulties. Call the number on the "for rent" sign and ask to speak with the owner. They may be quite pleased to hear from you. I suggest beginning with commercial real estate agents since it will provide you the quickest results. Once you've met every broker in town and are in need of additional deal flow, try using some of these other deal-finding methods.

Apply the Four Keys to Apartment Building Investment Immediately

Most real estate investors who are contemplating investing in apartment buildings face at least one of the following obstacles:

"I lack experience; thus, I will wait."

"I do not have the funds, therefore I will have to wait."

"I don't know how to begin (hence, I'll wait)"

"Because I do not know how to discover excellent offers, I will wait."

I hope you see how you can overcome each of these obstacles by: - educating yourself, using scripts, and building your team so you appear more experienced than you are and don't sound like a newbie; - raising money from others, - getting started by learning how to analyze deals and make 10-Minute Offers with confidence; and - building relationships with brokers who will provide you with all the deals you need.

Now that you are aware of the four strategies to overcoming each of these obstacles, you can immediately begin your road toward financial independence by investing in flats. No more excuses. You have all the resources necessary for success. Next, I will provide you with a detailed action plan, so you will know precisely what to do to complete your first sale within the next twelve months (or sooner). The Law of the First Deal will then set you on the road to retirement within three to five years.

PART III
THE FINANCIAL INDEPENDENCE BLUEPRINT: SEVEN STEPS TO QUITTING YOUR JOB IN THREE TO FIVE YEARS

CHAPTER 6
STEP 1: CALCULATE (AND DECREASE) YOUR LIFE SPENDING NUMBER

Remember the "ONE thing" need to achieve financial independence via real estate. That's correct... this is your first transaction. According to the Law of the First Deal, if you complete your first multifamily transaction (of any value), you will achieve financial independence within three to five years. But you'll never get there if you don't know how to reach that first bargain. For this reason, I created the Financial Freedom Blueprint, the most thorough and exclusive strategy for teaching you step-by-step how to become (permanently) financially free with real estate in the next three to five years.

The 7-step Financial Freedom Blueprint guides you from correctly establishing your objectives, to getting started, to closing your first sale, to achieving financial independence. This step-by-step plan has worked for me and hundreds of others before you, and it will work for you as well. Let's begin with the first phase, which is determining (and decreasing) your life spending number. Robert Kiyosaki describes financial independence in his book <u>Rich Dad Poor Dad</u> as the moment at which you can meet your living expenditures with passive income. This is known as the "Rat Race Number." After achieving this, you are financially independent and can do anything you desire, such as leave your work, travel more, spend more time with family, pursue non-profit goals, etc.

There are two approaches to reach your Rat Race Number: increase passive income and decrease costs. Let's first determine how to compute your Rat Race Number so that our objectives are crystal apparent. To get your Rat Race Number, you must determine what you spend NOW and what you might do to reduce those costs. What are your current expenditures? Start monitoring your expenditures immediately if you are not already doing so. It is fundamental to effective personal financial management. My family does this monthly for many years. Mint.com is a valuable resource. It is an online tool and mobile application that makes it very simple to monitor your spending and prevents you from going over budget. You may also monitor your spending using a spreadsheet.

I recommend keeping track of your costs for three months to determine your monthly spending average. How Can You Save Money? Next, examine each spending category and determine what you can eliminate. I'm aware that this is a tough step. We enjoy the way our life is! We're accustomed to the caramel macchiato each day. We adore our 1,500+ cable channels. We adore our brand-new automobiles and homes. I got it. I do too. But consider this: how strongly do you want financial independence? If you really want it, then could you live without some of your normal comforts? If you need assistance with this, I strongly suggest Financial Peace University by Dave Ramsey. This course assists you in determining your spending, developing a budget, eliminating debt, and saving for the future. You may do an online course or join a group near you, and it's quite reasonable.

Consider it in this manner: A decent rental property should leave you with at least $200 per month after costs. So for every $2

00 you save every month, it's roughly the same as acquiring one rental unit. If you could save $1,000 every month, that would be equivalent to constructing your own 10-unit apartment complex! Avoid skipping this step. Consider what costs you can eliminate and what adjustments you might make (and endure!) to save money. The lower your Rat Race Number, the quicker you will attain financial independence.

What are you willing to undertake to achieve your objectives?

What's Your Number in the Rat Race? Let's imagine you tracked your REAL monthly costs and made adjustments to cut them by 20% every month. And suppose you concluded that you could survive on $5,000 per month if you tightened your belt considerably. That's $60,000 each year. You could be thinking, yeah, but what about taxes? The wonderful thing about investing in real estate is that you'll likely be paying much less taxes (perhaps none at all) on your apartment building revenue. This is because the IRS permits you to depreciate the building's worth. This depreciation is included as a cost on your tax return (which decreases your taxable income) despite the fact that it is not a cash-flow-affecting item.

Real estate taxation is outside the scope of this book, but suffice it to say that your taxes on real estate income are significantly lower than on your W-2 income, and there's a good possibility you're not even paying taxes on that money. Consult your tax professional. I hope you get my argument on property taxes. For the sake of this experiment, let's say that your monthly living costs total $5,000. How Will You Obtain Access? For many of you, this may be the first time you're completing this activity. Isn't it eye-opening? After obtaining your Rat Race Number, the next concern is how you will get there. You now know that you need $5,000 in passive income per month. Which approach to real estate will get you there the quickest? If you're currently flipping properties, you know that there's nothing passive about it (I've flipped over twenty houses, so I have some experience with this!). So flipping properties is NOT going to be the type of activity that provides passive income. What about developing a portfolio of rentals? This surely counts as a source of passive income, so please tick the box. How many properties would be required to generate $5,000 per month? This depends on your market and how excellent of an investor you are. Let's imagine you're constantly able to earn $200 per month in cash flow (after expenditures, including vacancies and maintenance!) from your rental homes. That's terrific! But at $200 per month in passive income, you would need twenty-five residences to retire. That's a lot of homes. Do you have the funds for that? How long would it take for you to establish such a portfolio? Do you even want that many homes? Have you ever thought about this?

Don't Skip this Step!

You may be tempted to avoid this step since it is difficult and might possibly impact your life. But Step #1 of the Financial Freedom Blueprint is crucial because it may expedite your financial objectives, sometimes dramatically. As you may have learned from playing CASHFLOW 101, it is significantly more difficult for high-income earners (such as attorneys) to escape the rat race than for janitors. Even while the attorney has a bigger salary, his costs are also much higher, and it takes longer for passive income to pay them. It would have taken me a LOT longer to achieve financial independence if I hadn't reduced my home and begun living on a budget. So don't overlook this phase in your search for financial independence. As previously said, every $100 you save is equivalent to purchasing one rental unit.

If you estimated that you required one hundred units to replace your monthly income of $10,000 and you were able to lower your living expenditures by $2,000, it is as if you simply purchased twenty units. It is the "easiest" initial transaction since you have the greatest control.

Suddenly, you are 20% closer to accomplishing your financial objective. So immediately enroll in Dave Ramsey's Financial Peace University. With flats, you may reduce your living expenditures and increase your passive income. This is a potent combination. We can now go on to the second stage of the Financial Freedom Blueprint, which is to create your "Vision Map" so that you know where you're heading and how to get there.

Second step of Chapter 7: Complete Your Vision Map

In this stage, I want you to build a clear understanding of your objectives and a plan to accomplish them. While you should have objectives for many elements of your life (relationships, spirituality, health, etc.), for the sake of this exercise, I'm referring to goals connected to obtaining financial independence through real estate. The issue is that most individuals don't think they can become financially free with real estate since the very concept of it seems daunting. We all want to be successful real estate investors so that we may retire and do the things we REALLY want to do. To be successful, we are instructed to think large. Only if we imagine large can we genuinely accomplish greatness. That's because if we don't dream large, we're confined by our own experience, talents, and comfort zone. Thinking on a grand scale compels us to think creatively and outside of our comfort zone. It helps us consider what is conceivable rather than what is likely.

The issue with big-picture thinking arises when it is disconnected from concrete objectives that pave the road to achieving those lofty ambitions. In other words, you must think BIG while also having a small-scale PLAN, or at least enough of one to know what you should do next. My Vision Map Exercise enables me to link the dream to the strategy. This strategy combines "Vision" (i.e., big-picture thinking) with a blueprint (or plan) of how to get there. The map comprises of milestones throughout twelve months, ninety days, and this week.

Function of the Vision Map

You may develop a Vision Map for any aspect of your life: business/financial, health, relationships, entertainment (fun!), spirituality, giving, and any other area that's important to you. Write a "I am" statement for what you want to be, accomplish, or have in each aspect of your life. I recommend you to write them in the present tense, as this will help you imagine yourself achieving this objective. Assume, for instance, that your financial goal is to leave your work in three to five years by amassing multifamily apartments. You may have the following "I am" statement: I am fiscally independent. I no longer have to work for a living. This is your vision, your BIG IDEA. Next, you identify a goal with the major concept so that you can determine whether it has been accomplished. This objective is precise, quantifiable, and expressed in the present tense: By (such-and-such a date), I am passively generating $10,000 each month. If you are beginning from scratch, you may have no notion how you will achieve this objective. That is an EXCELLENT example of BIG thinking.

So far so wonderful. Next, you want to boil this down into a twelve- month objective, possibly something like this: I have closed on my first transaction (20 units), and it cash flows $3,500 each month. This is starting to become more real! Rather of focusing on a daunting monthly target of $10,000, you should concentrate on ONE thing: the first transaction, a 20-unit apartment complex.

Next, convert this twelve-month objective into a ninety-day objective. I prefer the ninety-day time period because it's long enough to accomplish something significant yet short enough to visualize yourself accomplishing the objective if you work hard. Something similar: In ninety days, I've assembled a team of property managers and bankers, met with 10 investors, assessed fifty transactions, and made twenty proposals. A goal that can be reached with effort. And, lastly, transform it into your objectives for THIS week, possibly like this: I talked with one property manager, spoke with one possible investor, and assessed five offers this week. Moreover, what you must do TODAY is now much clearer: I will contact one property manager today.

It is imperative that you think BIG, without a doubt. However, many individuals fail to link their expansive thinking with what they must accomplish TODAY, right now. And if you are unable to do so, you will feel overwhelmed and give up before you even begin. Therefore, avoid falling into the "think big" trap. Complete the Goal Map activity to clarify not just your vision but also your path to achieving it. Now that we know what we want (and don't want), the next stage in the Financial Freedom Blueprint is to: The Launch Preparation Sequence.

CHAPTER 7
THIRD STEP: PRE-LAUNCH SEQUENCE (THE FIRST 30 DAYS)

The Pre-Launch Sequence focuses on acquiring the basic skill set and self-assurance necessary to enter the world without sounding like a novice. I will demonstrate how to become a "experienced" multifamily investor in thirty days. Here is the week-by-week plan:

Week 1: Educate Yourself in Order to Avoid Sounding Like a Novice

In the first week, you will educate yourself. The difficulty is that the majority of individuals have no idea how to begin investing in apartment buildings or generating capital. They lack the expertise to do specific tasks, or they lack the scripts and equipment necessary to get started. Obviously, the answer is a solid system that teaches you how to analyze prospects and raise capital; this is essential. The objective is to accomplish it. So you learn the vocabulary, fundamental investment principles, and the actions necessary to complete your first trade. Don't get bogged down with classroom instruction; complete everything in the first week and then go on to week 2. Now that you have finished your "basic training," it is imperative that you have a thorough understanding of your first transaction. And that is exactly what we will do next.

Week 2: Clarify Your Initial Contract

This week, I want you to become crystal clear on your first transaction. The issue is that the majority of individuals miss this phase and pursue opportunities without having a clear image of what their first deal should look like. As a consequence, they either make a deal that is too tiny or chase a transaction that is too large before failing to accomplish any agreement. If we properly outline our initial transaction, we will be able to imagine what it will look like. If we can see it, it becomes more real, and the more real it is, the more probable it is that we will reach that crucial objective along the route to financial independence. Clarity in your initial contract is crucial. Your initial transaction should be relevant and realizable. Meaningful in that it should enable you to make quantifiable progress toward your financial independence objective. Typically, this implies that it must be as large as feasible. Meaning that, although your offer should be as large as feasible, it must also be realizable within the following twelve months. Everyone's first transaction will be somewhat unique. It involves an honest assessment of your financial condition and ambitions. If your Rat Race Number is $10,000 each month, there is a greater likelihood that you have funds to invest and that you know other individuals with money to invest. In light of the fact that you can gather $200,000 in the next three to six months, a 25-unit apartment complex may be an appropriate initial investment. Alternatively, if your Rat Race Number is $5,000, you may have little funds and be less likely to meet other wealthy folks. If this is the case, a duplex or four-plex might be a good initial investment. If you choose an unattainable first offer, you will likely give up. If your initial investment is little, it may take you longer than three to five years to achieve financial independence. Remember that the "best" initial contract is one that is both significant and realizable within the following year.

Where Should You Invest?

In addition to the magnitude of the first transaction, the location of the first deal is the second most crucial question to address. In general, we want a rising market that may provide a satisfactory return. This disqualifies cities like San Francisco and New York City because, despite their economic growth, their low yields make it impossible for the typical entrepreneur to provide an acceptable return for investors. What happens if you reside in one of these regions? The answer is to search beyond your region. It is not difficult. Geography should not be an issue or an excuse nowadays. You can accomplish the job electronically since so much is accessible online, and if you must go in person, you can reach almost every U.S. location inside a five-hour trip. The only reason you wouldn't leave your comfort zone is because you want to remain inside it. And do we develop while remaining in our comfort zone? I believe that you know the solution. Consequently, the following issue is: how do you identify the best region to invest in?

How to Select the Best Neighborhoods for Multifamily Investments with Confidence

Where to search is one of the greatest obstacles when starting started in multifamily investment. With the market being as heated as it is, many investors are searching for opportunities outside of their immediate area. But where should one search? How do you approach it? This is not a trivial decision, since the location you pick will be where you spend many hours searching for bargains, assembling teams, and maintaining the property. The evaluation technique is based on the following criteria:

- Look for regions that you like. Start by selecting a region that you like, or at least one where you wouldn't mind spending time. Perhaps you have relatives and friends living there, or you just like the location. Consider the travel logistics as well. Is it a reasonable drive or flight to get there? For instance, I want to be able to reach the destination in less than two hours by direct flight.

- Search for "high-yield" regions. If you are in between), then you are aware that the multifamily housing market is sizzling. When others are prepared to overpay, it will be more difficult to locate great discounts. This might necessitate a search in less desirable towns or secondary marketplaces, which may be off the main route yet give larger returns. Those in "high-yield" locations are valued less in relation to their revenue than properties in other places (i.e., their cash-on-cash returns are higher, as well as their Cap Rates).

- Look for places with "strong growth." You want to invest in regions where employment is expanding, and ideally, you want that employment to be as diverse as possible. This will help prevent what occurred during the recession in regions dependent on a small number of sectors.

Using three really valuable reports, I'd want to be more explicit about how to apply these criteria.

Three Reports to Help You Identify the Right Region

Here are three free publications to assist you in evaluating investment markets.

National Apartment Report by Marcus & Millichap. To get access to this report, please visit their website and register for a free account. The study rates the nation's leading metropolitan regions based on the following very essential criteria:

- Trends in vacancy and rental rates

- Sales trends

-Capitalization rate and yield

-Employment expansion

The IRR Perspective Report. The IRR Viewpoint report is another valuable publication accessible on the IRR website. This report depicts major cities on the "Market Cycle" graph, from "Recovery/Expansion" through "Hyper Supply" to "Recession." And it does so for a variety of asset types (e.g., multifamily, retail, office, etc.) and significant cities throughout the nation. The report displays graphically where the main markets are in the "up-and-down" market cycle. It is intriguing that certain markets are still "recovering." Surprisingly, there are also a substantial number of markets that are growing but not yet hot (i.e., "expanding"). You should ideally seek out markets in the Recovery and Expansion cycles and avoid properties in the Hyper-Supply and Recession cycles.

The Milken Report on the Highest-Performing Cities. Downloadable from Milken Institute, the Milken Best Performing Cities Study is the third helpful report. This research assesses 400 cities—200 major and 200 small—based on their employment growth and provides in-depth profiles of the top-ranked cities. This enables you to see your city's position on the list and its current trend. If your city is near the bottom of the list and declining, it may be prudent to exercise caution before investing there. Alternatively, if your city is expanding and the trend is favorable, it may be a good time to invest there.

Where to Begin: Putting Everything together

This is a great deal of information, and you may feel entirely overwhelmed by the prospect of selecting one topic from several options. Why not begin with the IRR Perspective report? Create a list of cities inside the Recovery or Expansion Market Cycles. Then, cross-reference the High-Yield Markets in the Marcus & Millichap study with the Markets with the Most Anticipated Employment Growth. Add them to the locations where you wouldn't mind spending time, and you may have a list of three to five cities. Then, using the remaining data, narrow down each of these cities and choose your top three.

These three studies will assist you in identifying markets where you may find bargains. If you can combine strong employment growth with an expanding market cycle and high capitalization rates, you have a great mix for investing in that market. Keep in mind, however, that real estate investment is still very local; just because a city has a low rating in the Best Cities list does not imply that a portion of the city is not expanding. And vice versa. So, these figures should be taken with a grain of salt. Nonetheless, this process in conjunction with these three reports is a good instrument for identifying a place for your next multifamily investment.

Week 3: Examine Five Transactions to Gain Confidence

This week, we aim to gain a head start on improving the ability to assess agreements fast and precisely. After analyzing at least five agreements, you will no longer seem like a novice, you will be able to make offers more swiftly and precisely, and your level of confidence will improve significantly. If you are able to do so, brokers will return your phone calls and investors will consent to a meeting. We have previously discussed analysis Refer back to Secret #3: How to Analyze Bargains and Make Offers in 10 Minutes if you need a refresher on deals. To examine a transaction, you will need a reliable financial model. You may create your own spreadsheet, search the Internet for one, or buy my Syndicated Deal Analyzer.

Find the best one, but be certain:

- It is designed to analyze multifamily properties.

- Purchase and exit assumptions are included.

-It can provide ten-year financial predictions; -It includes investment returns; and -The program is modifiable so that the model may be customized.

Once a solid financial model has been developed, it is time to start to work. Here are some methods for obtaining deals to analyze:

LoopNet: Create a free account at loopnet.com and search for multifamily properties. On LoopNet, there will be no scarcity of properties! You may have to contact the broker in order to get the financials.

- MLS: You may also locate multifamily listings on realtor.com (where homes are advertised).

It does not matter how fantastic the bargain is or whether it meets your initial deal criterion for this phase. Find and evaluate a bargain, any deal. Repeat five times. If you contact brokers and they refuse to call you back or provide you their marketing materials, you should go elsewhere. This stage does NOT include contacting brokers; rather, it involves assessing transactions. Okay? Okay...move on to the next week.

Week 4: Complete the Sample Deal Fundraising Package

Create a Sample Offer Package using a previously evaluated deal from Week 3 that fulfills the requirements for your first deal from Week 2. Refer to Secret No. 1: Raise All the Money You Need for Your First Deal for a reminder and instructions on how to obtain a template on How to Create the Sample Deal Package. Not only is the Sample Offer Package an essential fundraising tool, but it also helps you imagine your first deal. Visualization is used by elite athletes and taught by renowned coaches such as Tony Robbins and others. Why? Because it works. The more your ability to envision something, the more tangible it becomes. And the more your belief, the more real it becomes. And the sooner it becomes a reality, the more you believe in it.

Congratulations! The first thirty days of the Pre-Launch Sequence have passed. You've educated yourself so that you don't seem like a beginner; you've clarified your first transaction; you've boosted your abilities and confidence by learning to assess offers; and you've prepared the Sample Deal Package to raise capital. You are now prepared to enter the marketplace as an apartment building entrepreneur. Time to launch!

CHAPTER 8
STEP #4: LAUNCH (THE NEXT 60 DAYS)

During the Pre-Launch Sequence, you honed your critical thinking abilities and boosted your self-assurance so that you can approach brokers and investors without seeming like a novice. The Launch Step is more about action and less about result. The most crucial aspect of this stage is maintaining continuous exercise to form new habits. Here are the three weekly activities you should perform:

- Activity #1: Conduct an analysis and make offers

- Activity Number Two: Meet with prospective investors

- Activity No. 3: Form your A-Team

Let's investigate each action in further depth:

Activity No. 1: Evaluate and Make Proposals

To continue creating trust and generate a transaction pipeline, it will be necessary to locate and evaluate opportunities. You may aim to complete five transactions every week, or one per day. Adjust this quantity according to your available time. Since with any kind of real estate investment, the more the quantity, the better, as this is a numbers game. When I say examine five offers, it entails creating a 10-Minute Offer for each of the five deals. This implies you're responding back to the broker with something like, "The asking price won't work for me, and here's why, and here's the price that would work—is there any flexibility?" In order to regularly accomplish this step each week, you will need to contact brokers. This step was discussed in Secret No. 4: The Number One Way to Find the Best Deals, so consult that section if necessary. Keep in mind that consistency and perseverance are crucial.

Activity #2 is to meet with prospective investors.

In addition to assessing transactions in order to construct a deal pipeline, you must also construct a pipeline of investors. If you can have verbal commitments from investors prior to signing a contract, you may confidently make proposals. The method of discovering and engaging with possible investors has previously been explained in Secret #1: Raise All the Money You Need for Your First Deal. Now classroom time is gone; it's time to really do it! A fair weekly aim would be to meet with one possible investor. To organize a weekly meeting with a possible investor, you must construct a mind map and contact 10 potential investors each week. Similar to the preceding task, consistency is crucial. Always communicate with prospective investors. Once the relationship is established, request a meeting with them to explore prospective investments. Do not worry excessively about the result. Talk to and meet with everyone who will offer you their time, regardless of their financial situation. It requires practice and confidence-building. Simply do it.

Activity #3: Form Your All-Star Team

Long before you have your first transaction under contract, you should have identified these additional members of your team:

- Property manager - Landlord/tenant lawyer - Real estate lawyer - Securities and Exchange Commission lawyer - Commercial lenders and brokers

- Real estate inspector - Valuer - Insurance agent

Your success as an investor in apartment buildings is contingent on the caliber of your crew. Therefore, avoid shortcuts and construct the finest team possible. Referrals are the greatest method for recruiting new team members. Yes, you may do an Internet search and visit the appropriate association's website, but I prefer suggestions. In fact, you prefer recommendations to individuals with whom your connections have really transacted business, so they can directly testify for their credibility. Commercial real estate agents provide one of the finest opportunities for recommendations. Request the names of reputable experts with whom they have done business. Ask EVERY person you speak with for a recommendation. If you are dealing with a broker, contact a property manager for a reference. When conversing with a property management, request a recommendation to an insurance agent, etc.

I suggest that you log your activities using the following columns in a spreadsheet:

-Name and contact information - Type of team member (e.g., property manager, mortgage broker, etc.) so that you can filter by team member type easily

- Who directed you to this individual?

- Activity Log: date with conversation and/or email description

The most crucial team member to recruit as soon as possible.

The property manager is by far the most crucial member of your team to hire well in advance of signing your first transaction. During the process of due diligence, he or she may assist you with rental comparables, vacancy rates, and inspections. Avoid this predicament at all costs: you locate a great 21-unit property with strong potential, sign a Letter of Intent, and successfully raise capital. The thought comes to you that maybe you should have a coach or mentor evaluate the agreement with you, and he asks you questions such as "How do you know that the rentals are $100 below market?" and "Why do you believe you can charge the renters back for the utilities?" You inform him that you verified the rents on rentometer.com and they were $100 more than the current rates. Oh, you were also uncertain about the second question. Even with a superb instrument like rentometer.com, an armchair rental analysis is insufficient at this point of the game. Either you must do your own rental study by phoning or visiting comparable apartment complexes, or you must be able to depend on a competent local property manager who can validate your assumptions.

If you do not have a property manager who is prepared to assist you at this time, you are flying blind, particularly if you are investing in an unfamiliar location.

The idea is to identify at least one property manager long before you put a home under contract, someone you can contact on if you go near to securing a deal.

At this step, they may assist you by driving by the property and providing input on what they saw. They can advise you on rents, customary practices (such as charging back rentals), and general guidelines for calculating rent expenses. Later, during due diligence, they continue to be a valuable resource by viewing the property alongside you, calculating repair costs, and generating pro forma financials. Avoid skipping this step! Thus, you will be ready to hit the ground running when you are close to closing a sale!

At this point in the lesson, I usually get at least one of the following three questions: - How many transactions do I need to examine in order to obtain one? As stated before, transactions will not fall into your lap. Many individuals believe that by making many offers, they would get a discount. Experience simply doesn't justify this. I anticipate a ratio closer to 100 to 10 to 1: for every 100 projects you assess, you will file a LOI for 10, and ultimately close 1 transaction. If you are reviewing two offers every week, it would take you about one year to close a single transaction. If you want to close your first transaction as fast as possible, plan out the amount of offers you must examine each week, and then take action!

- How much time do I need to devote to be successful? Let me begin by stating that every single person I know who became a full-time investor began out with a full-time job. If you can devote 10 hours a week to your endeavor, you will be successful. This may include one hour in the morning or evening for analyzing opportunities and making offers, and another hour throughout the day for making phone calls. We make time for things that we want or like. If you do not make the time, you do not want financial independence. There is nothing wrong with it; just ask yourself what you want, and you will discover how you are spending your time.

- How do I proceed with action? Is it feasible that your lack of progress is due to your hectic schedule? You don't know where to start? Are you overwhelmed by the whole concept? Then I recommend that you begin by taking TINY action. Not a GIANT action. Tiny action consists of doing TINY tasks every day until they yield MASSIVE outcomes in the future. Could you devote an additional thirty minutes every day to real estate? Could you purchase a notepad, write down the following three tasks, and then carry them out? IF YOU DO THESE TWO SMALL THINGS EVERY DAY FOR THE NEXT 30 DAYS, YOU WILL BE AMAZED AT HOW FAR YOU HAVE COME.

Conclusion

The Launch Phase is all about constant action to develop the routines of researching prospects (and making bids), interacting with possible investors, and creating a staff. It is not about the result. Quantity trumps quality. This indicates that you may be studying an offer that you already know will fail. That's OK.

Regardless, analyze it and make an offer. You may be meeting with a buddy who you know doesn't have any money to invest. That's alright. Utilize this as a chance to practice.

If you incline toward analysis/paralysis, then it's time to stop reading another book or attending another seminar, and it's time to take action. If you're a perfectionist, you may find this stage challenging since you're attempting to have everything prepared before finding a broker. Before you book your first investor meeting, you may want to have your website and business cards completed. You do not need perfection; action is required. Don't overthink things; simply take action. Take one TINY action every day.

CHAPTER 9
STEP 5: CONSTRUCT YOUR PIPELINE

I told you that the Launch Step is more concerned with action than with result. Nonetheless, if you put in the effort, you will inevitably achieve success without even trying: you will have a pipeline of business and investors, as well as a team on the ground that is ready to go. The "Pipeline Step" entails continuing to make offers and raise funds in order to grow your pipeline. And the larger your pipeline, the quicker you will close your first transaction. In addition to making bids, you'll face mental obstacles in what I term "the cemetery of apartment building investment."

Survival Strategies for Apartment Building Investing in the "Graveyard"

A few months later, the entrepreneur's enthusiasm starts to fade, and he or she feels dissatisfied by the seeming lack of development. Consequently, many abandon their pursuit of financial independence for two basic reasons:

- #1: Lack of community and support - #2: Delays, difficulties, and obstacles

Working with hundreds of students, I've discovered that these sentiments of despondency impact every entrepreneur at least once, if not more than once. The crucial factor is how you react to them. Let's examine each of them in further detail so that you're in the greatest position to manage and overcome them.

Reason #1: Lack of community and support

It is a lonely sport to be a real estate entrepreneur pursuing your first apartment building transaction. There is a good chance that you do not have a single friend or family member who has accomplished your goal. In fact, many of your friends and family members consider you insane and do little to support you on your path. Then there is the dilemma of who to ask when you have a query. Even the finest training or seminar will not be able to cover every potential scenario, since every transaction is unique. Whom can you consult if you have a question? Are you purchasing wisely? Are you too eager to do business? What should be done about the mold problem that was discovered during due diligence? Many of these questions might be paralyzing if you do not have a support system. The key to achieving success in this phase is to get assistance and join a network of other entrepreneurs.

Find a partner for accountability.

Only 10 individuals out of one hundred who attend a session will take action. If you are one of the 90% of individuals who don't naturally finish what they start, you will need an accountability partner, someone who will motivate and hold you responsible. This someone may be a spouse, a close friend, or someone you pay (like a coach or mentor). It is immaterial which of them you seek out, but you must identify yourself with a person of this kind. Otherwise, your efforts will eventually fizzle out. Therefore, ensure that you have a partner for accountability.

Surround yourself with like-minded individuals.

Ensure that you are surrounded by a network of entrepreneurs working toward the same objectives who can provide assistance. On good days, you want to share your accomplishments. But who can fully comprehend and value your accomplishments? And on bad days, you need someone to reassure you that everything will be alright, that your efforts are meaningful, and that you should keep going. Who really comprehends what we endure? True, very few individuals, particularly our friends and family. You must thus seek out a network of like-minded businesses. Again, the kind of community you have is less important than the fact that you are a member of one. Community might function as a mastermind group. Perhaps you form one with the folks you meet at boot camp, or you may pay to join one. A virtue or online community is a fantastic and often more practical alternative to in-person interaction. Paid or unpaid, in-person or online, you must be a member of a community. This will guarantee the longevity of your acts and the ultimate success of your endeavor.

3. Identify a mentor

Elite athletes use coaches. Professional actors have coaches. Even the most successful executives have coaches. Have you hired a coach? If not, you will struggle to attain your objectives. It will take longer and you will make many more errors than required. You will confront circumstances you have never encountered, and a mentor may assist you in navigating these uncharted seas. You may find a mentor who is willing to meet with you periodically for lunch and answer your queries. You may be able to discover investors with similar levels of expertise in apartment buildings via your local REIA or by asking about. I urge that you assemble a "board of advisors" comprised of more seasoned investors; they are helpful. However, I've discovered that "volunteer" mentors seldom provide the kind of assistance you need, particularly in the beginning. Therefore, I believe it is advisable to engage a coach to assist you with your first sale. Every successful real estate entrepreneur has had a mentor or adviser, if not a paid coach. Not addressing the problem of assistance is one of the two primary reasons individuals abandon their pursuit of their first apartment building transaction.

Locate an accountability partner, create or join a network of like-minded individuals, and find an experienced mentor or coach. If you follow these recommendations, your chances of success will increase dramatically.

Reason Two: Delays, Obstacles, and Difficulties

Around three months after a person decides to invest in apartment buildings, the initial excitement wears off and they grow upset since they have not yet closed a contract or obtained capital. And, honestly, it is more labor than they anticipated. They may believe to oneself, "This multifamily thing doesn't seem to work."

Or maybe it works for others but not me. Here are some suggestions for coping with these days of uncertainty and despondency.

The first piece of advice is to revisit your why.

Do you recall the Vision Map Exercise? Now is the moment to reread your Vision Map and reflect on why you embarked on this insane trip in the first place. Was it to leave your job? To alleviate the continual burden of providing for your family? Why was this significant? To recover control of your time to do anything you wanted, whenever you desired, and with whoever you desired? And why was this significant? Was it to spend more time with your growing children? To enhance your connection with your partner? To travel more? Think back to the moment when you chose to begin multifamily investment, whatever the reason may have been. What agony were you attempting to escape? What more did you want for yourself and your family? If this suggestion fails to motivate you, repeat the Vision Map Exercise. However, this time was different. Invest time in it. Consider it deeply. Include your partner and relatives. One of my favorite quotations is from Tony Robbins: "Your destiny is formed in your moments of choosing." When a person sincerely chooses something, I believe action is the only potential consequence. When a person is inactive and I inquire more, I discover that they have not made a final decision. They may claim they want something, but they are deceiving themselves and others. This is why it's crucial that you decide, right now, whether you want to alter your life or you want to have the same life you have now now this time next year. If you do, that's good, but if you don't, you should immediately determine you want a new life. Once you do so, you will discover that taking action comes effortlessly. The universe will provide you your deepest desires. I have seen it in my own life and the lives of countless others. But you have to decide.

Tip No. 2: Maintain perspective.

Investing in apartment buildings is a difficult endeavor. It is certainly beneficial, but it is difficult. The desired outcomes (replacement your income) cannot be obtained in thirty days or less. No, you must persevere every week for three to five years before you can leave your work and pursue your passion. This may seem like a very long period, but consider that your retirement plan is just three to five years long. Your retirement plan spans just three to five years, when the average plan spans over forty. Isn't that much better? Consequently, if you are contemplating quitting after three months of apartment building investment, examine the time frame. You are on a three- to five-year retirement plan, therefore it is obvious that three months will not enough. However, you are aware that your retirement timeline is far superior and quicker than that of 99.9% of the population, therefore it is absolutely worthwhile.

Okay, enough with the whining. Return to executing the plan!

Recognize and appreciate your (little) achievements.

In my experience dealing with kids, it is common for them to be unaware of their development. They are so intent on closing their first sale (as they should be!) that they feel disheartened when it does not occur within the first few months. In actuality, they have made a great deal of progress, and it is essential to acknowledge this by enjoying the minor victories. Here are some instances of little accomplishments that you should celebrate (along with their significance):

- You evaluated ten transactions: This is significant because it reveals that you are unable to escape it. Anyone can evaluate a few transactions, but 10 demonstrates perseverance. Good for you! Another reason why this milestone is significant is that after examining around 10 agreements, your confidence level grows dramatically, making this a significant achievement.

- You have sent your first Letter of Intent: If you've read thus far, you're aware that everytime you examine a transaction, you're also making an informal 10-Minute Offer. If the seller responds with a counteroffer or requests that you put your offer in writing, you next send a Letter of Intent. In order to be requested to submit a LOI, it is assumed that you have submitted a dozen or more 10-Minute Offers, which is a tremendous achievement in and of itself. Then you persuaded a broker to take you seriously, indicating that you likely have a formidable team and a greater degree of confidence. In other words, being requested to submit a letter of intent is a monumental achievement that should be celebrated lavishly.

- You've had your first investor meeting: If you've persuaded an investor to meet with you for an hour to talk investing, you must have gone out to at least a dozen individuals in your network and had several discussions about your apartment building investment goals. This first investor meeting required much planning and action; sound the bell!

- Your squad is assembled: Have you conducted interviews and selected your preferred property manager and business mortgage broker? If so, then this is a monumental achievement. These two team members will be crucial when analyzing deals and making proposals. Without them, you would be blind as a bat. Commend and celebrate this achievement!

- You received your first investment commitment: Your brother-in-law said that he would wager $40,000? Don't brush over this; it's important! Not only did a great deal of work precede your achievement, but you also convinced someone to invest with you. You are being taken seriously. Nice work! In addition, this first investment enhances your confidence as you approach further investors. Now, it is lot simpler to locate a second and third investor than it was to find the first. You are now well on your way to raising ALL the funds necessary for your first transaction. Keep it up!

- You have signed your first agreement: Even if you have a signed letter of intent (LOI), it does not guarantee that you will get a formal contract. A letter of intent is not a legally binding document, and many brokers and sellers use it as such during negotiations with their actual buyer. Frequently, the devil is in the details, and you and the seller may not agree with the terms of the contract as they are written. Contracting a transaction also signifies that the seller is confident in you, your team, and your capacity to close. This landmark is monumental. Bring the family to supper! Continue with It! Awareness is the first step in surviving the "graveyard of apartment building investment." Anticipate uncertainty and discouragement when you encounter setbacks, difficulties, and delays. This is when a partner in accountability or a mentor becomes essential, as they will assist you through times of uncertainty and despair. They will put these emotions in perspective, remind you of your objectives, emphasize the progress you've already achieved, and urge you to continue. The good news is that if you can get through the next three months, you'll be OK. Simply be conscious of it, surround yourself with positive support, and continue to go ahead.

CHAPTER 10
STEP 5: PUTTING EVERYTHING TOGETHER

If you remember just one thing from the book, let it be this: "The ONE THING for reaching financial independence via real estate is to concentrate on your first multifamily venture." And, student, why is it the solitary thing? The reason for this is the Law of the First Deal, which states: "The first multifamily transaction (of ANY SIZE) leads in financial independence within three to five years." You are now familiar with the Four Secrets of Successful Apartment Building Investors. You've discovered:

-How to be regarded seriously while having little experience

-How to assess transactions and make offers within 10 minutes (and more)

-How to get the capital necessary for your first contract (and beyond)

-The number one method for finding the finest discounts

Then, I shared with you the Seven Steps of the Financial Freedom Blueprint: 1. Calculate and lower your Rat Race Number

2. Complete your vision map

3. Prepare for the launch using a 30-day pre-launch sequence

Launch your company by assessing opportunities, meeting with investors, and assembling a team.

5. Build your transaction and investor pipeline

6. Sign your first contract

Utilize the Law of the First Deal to attain (permanent) financial independence.

And if you want even quicker results, you may accelerate the Financial Freedom Blueprint with one of the following techniques:

- Buy small - Partner to expedite your first transaction

- Make passive investments - Raise funds

I hope you can now understand how to get started with apartment complexes immediately, even if you don't have experience or your own money. You are now aware of the talents to prioritize and the plan to follow. Get your first transaction under wraps so you can use the Law of the First Deal and take your first steps toward achieving financial independence via real estate!

Thank you for reading my book. Thank you for learning to take control of your life. Here's to your freedom!

One Last Ask

Could I please ask you to leave a review for this book on Amazon? It means a lot. Thanks.

Made in the USA
Las Vegas, NV
18 November 2023

81055802R00059